Happily
Ever
After

Finding Grace in the
Messes of Marriage

30

DEVOTIONS

FOR

COUPLES

Happily Ever After: Finding Grace in the Messes of Marriage

Published for Desiring God by
CruciformPress

Print/PDF ISBN: 978-1-941114-23-0
Mobipocket ISBN: 978-1-941114-24-7
ePub ISBN: 978-1-941114-25-4

Contents

CONTENTS

Preface

Once upon a time . . .

Perhaps you felt like that's how *your* relationship was starting. You met and began talking, spending time together, learning about each other. You fell in love and were engaged. Maybe even the wedding planning and ceremony all went great. And many a couple—though not all—have had their joy-filled, storybook honeymoon.

But if you've been married longer than a week or two, you know how the hard realities of life in a fallen age can come crashing in. Marriage between sinners does have its messes—not just troubles outside your marriage to navigate together, but messes created *in* your marriage, by you and your spouse. You may have had your season of "once upon a time," but soon you realize that *this* marriage, in *this* world, is not yet your "happily ever after."

We want to help. We believe that God designed marriage not primarily as an obstacle, a trial to be endured though clenched teeth, but as a pointer and springboard to your greatest joy. Yes, rich joys can be tasted in this life, but the greatest joys are still to come. God didn't design marriage to be your storybook ending, but a fresh beginning, to help get you ready for the true "happily ever after" when together we see our great Bridegroom face to face.

You may have noticed that marriage is a hotly con-
tested topic today. Not only are many forces aggressively
trying to redefine its very essence, but the complexities
of life in the twenty-first century add stresses and strains
that push countless couples to the breaking point. It
may be more important than ever to revisit what God
has clearly revealed about marriage. If we're to have any
strong hopes that marriage may actually help our journey
through this fallen world—rather than make it all the
more treacherous—we desperately need to know what the
designer of marriage himself has to say about this unique
and uniquely significant institution.

In the pages ahead, we have compiled thirty brief
daily readings for you and your spouse to go through
together. We've chosen these especially with newlywed
and younger couples in mind, but the content is timeless
and we hope many veteran couples, and even engaged
couples, may find this material inspiring and appropriately
challenging.

These pages understandably include much emphasis on the things that make marriage unique: the
God-ordained context for sexual expression, the particular roles God has assigned to husbands and wives,
and the particular challenges that typically crop up in a
relationship of such multi-layered intimacy. And we've
tried to cover a breadth of subjects—from sexuality, to
husband-and-wife dynamics, to conflict resolution, to
growing in holiness. Also, in several places we have tried
to create a certain topical progression from one day to
another where that seems beneficial.

That said, we recognize that no series of short devo-
tionals can cover all the bases, and lay out all the implica-

tions, of the many profound passages of Scripture relating
to marriage. After all, marriage is a special institution
in God's kingdom, yet at the same time a means to the
larger end of glorifying our Creator and Savior by putting
the beauty of Christ and his church on display before a
watching world. We would not want these brief readings
to replace a larger, more thorough study of marriage, but
serve as an inspiring and clarifying supplement. Of the
many good marriage texts, we'd recommend John Piper's
This Momentary Marriage: A Parable of Permanence, and
also encourage you to browse desiringGod.org for articles,
sermons, and more.

In an effort to try to get you and your spouse moving
in the direction of practical application, each devotional
includes a small section called "Talk about It" to spark
discussion and action ideas for you to enjoy with your
partner.

May God be pleased to make these readings powerful in your marriage, as you seek to follow Jesus together
and serve each other toward the great "happily ever after"
that marriage is designed to anticipate.

Contributors

FRANCIS CHAN is a pastor in San Francisco and is actively planting churches in the Bay Area. He is author of *Crazy Love: Overwhelmed by a Relentless God*. He and his wife, Lisa, have four children and live in San Francisco.

JASMINE HOLMES is a wife, author, and foodie. She studied English literature and has served as a writing teacher at an inner-city classical school. She and her husband, Phillip, are parents of a newborn son.

DAVID MATHIS is executive editor of desiringGod.org and a pastor of Cities Church, Minneapolis, Minnesota. He is author of *Habits of Grace: Enjoying Jesus through the Spiritual Disciplines*. He and his wife, Megan, have three children.

JOHN PIPER is founder and teacher of desiringGod.org and chancellor of Bethlehem College & Seminary in Minneapolis, Minnesota. He is author of more than fifty books, including *This Momentary Marriage: A Parable of Permanence*. He and his wife, Noël, have five children and twelve grandchildren.

STACY REAOCH is a wife and mother of four. She enjoys ministering to women through Bible studies and discipleship at Three Rivers Grace Church, where her husband, Ben, is pastor. They live in Pittsburgh, Pennsylvania.

ADRIEN SEGAL lives in Minneapolis, Minnesota, with her husband, Rick. They are members of Bethlehem Baptist Church and work with Bethlehem College & Seminary. They have four sons and two grandchildren.

MARSHALL SEGAL is managing editor of desiringGod.org and author of the forthcoming book *Not Yet Married: The Pursuit of Joy in Singleness and Dating*. Marshall and his wife, Faye, live in Minneapolis and are expecting their first child.

JOSH SQUIRES serves as the pastor of counseling and congregational care at First Presbyterian Church in Columbia, South Carolina, where he lives with his wife, Melanie, and their four children.

KIM CASH TATE is a wife, mom, blogger, and author of several books, including, most recently, *Hidden Blessings*. She and her husband, Bill, live in Saint Louis, Missouri.

P. J. TIBAYAN is pastor of First Southern Baptist Church in Bellflower, California, where he lives with his wife, Frances, and their five children. He blogs at gospelize.me and helps lead The Gospel Coalition Los Angeles Regional Chapter and the Los Angeles Southern Baptist Association.

DONALD S. WHITNEY is a husband, father, and professor of biblical spirituality at The Southern Baptist Theological Seminary in Louisville, Kentucky. He is author of *Spiritual Disciplines for the Christian Life*, and most recently *Praying the Bible*.

DOUGLAS WILSON is pastor of Christ Church in Moscow, Idaho, and author of numerous books, including *Reforming Marriage* and *How to Exasperate Your Wife: And Other Short Essays for Men*. He and his wife, Nancy, have three children and numerous grandchildren.

NANCY DEMOSS WOLGEMUTH is founder of Revive Our Hearts, a ministry calling women to revival and true biblical womanhood. She is author of eighteen books and hosts two daily radio programs, *Revive Our Hearts* and *Seeking Him*. She is married to Robert and writes at the True Woman blog.

1

The Goal of Marriage
Is Not Marriage

FRANCIS CHAN

Do you not know that in a race all the runners run, but only one receives the prize? So run that you may obtain it.

—1 Corinthians 9:24

Because divorce runs so rampant even in the church, it makes sense that we tend to overcompensate by emphasizing marriage more than Scripture does. But by doing so, we may be hurting marriages rather than helping them.

Couples can all too easily become self-centered, rather than mission-focused. Singles who once radically served Jesus may now spend their days merely improving and enjoying their marriage. Other couples may quarrel incessantly and spend their days in counseling and despair. Either way, they become virtually worthless for kingdom purposes.

It doesn't have to be this way. This is why Paul wrote 1 Corinthians 7: "I say this for your own benefit, not to lay any restraint upon you, but to promote good order and to secure your undivided devotion to the Lord" (1 Cor. 7:35).

The goal is "undivided devotion to the Lord." Meditate on those words. Remember that the Bible is not a book about marriage; it is a book about God. The best thing we can do with our brief lives is to devote ourselves to him and his mission. This is the goal. And marriage can actually help us achieve this goal. That's why Paul encourages marriage for those who are tempted sexually. A healthy marriage helps to prevent temptations that would destroy our effectiveness. But remember that whether married or single, the goal is to be completely devoted to God. Marriage can be used as a means of improving our devotion to Jesus. Let's not get it backwards and think of him as the means of improving our marriages.

We don't have time to fight, nor to settle down. We are in pursuit of a prize (1 Cor. 9:24–27). We are trying to make as many disciples as possible (Matt. 28:18–20), at as much depth as possible. There will be plenty of time to celebrate after we cross the finish line. For now, we just keep running.

Talk about It

Have you observed what seems to be an overemphasis on marriage in the church? Discuss with your spouse how valuing marriage too highly will actually lead to hurting your marriage rather than helping it.

2

Seeing Jesus on the Stage of Marriage

P. J. TIBAYAN

*Husbands, love your wives, as Christ loved the church
and gave himself up for her, that he might sanctify her,
having cleansed her by the washing of water with the word.*
—Ephesians 5:25–26

He sacrifices, she submits. He leads, she follows. He initiates, she affirms. He reflects Jesus, she reflects Jesus.

The greatest privilege in marriage is reflecting our Savior. And in God's design, the privilege is equally great even though Jesus is reflected differently and uniquely by a husband and his wife.

Seeing Jesus in a Husband

He reflects Jesus. "Husbands, love your wives, as Christ loved the church and gave himself up for her, that he might sanctify her, having cleansed her by the washing of water with the word" (Eph. 5:25–26). Husbands are to love their wives. To love is to desire, plan, and act for the ultimate good of the beloved. So the husband must know what's best for his wife—God himself. Then he must plan, desire, and act to bring her to a greater knowledge and *enjoyment* of God.

The husband is called to reflect the sacrificial love of Jesus by dying to himself—his sin, selfishness, and personal interests—and instead enlarging his interests to include his bride's joy in God. That means dying to any ambition to be God in his wife's heart, and dying to his preferences when putting hers above his own will not lead to sin. In this sacrificial love, the wife will see a reflection of the Messiah as she looks at her man. And this love breeds trust.

The husband also reflects Jesus by washing his wife with the water of God's word. His goal is her holiness— her obedience to and satisfaction in her heavenly Father. So he speaks God's words to her, reads the Bible with her, and gently disagrees with and graciously rebukes her when she sins. He confesses his sin to her and repents according to God's word. In his unswerving allegiance to Scripture, the husband echoes Jesus's refrain, "It is written" (Matt. 4:4, 7, 10).

Seeing Jesus in a Wife

She reflects Jesus, too. "Wives, submit to your own husbands, as to the Lord. For the husband is the head of the wife even as Christ is the head of the church" (Eph. 5:22–23). The wife reflects Jesus by submitting to her husband as her head.

How? Paul teaches us that Jesus is under the headship of the Father (see 1 Cor. 11:3). Although fully God, Jesus humbled himself by becoming a human (Phil. 2:6–7). When asking his Father for the cup (symbolizing his impending death in our place) to be passed from him, he concluded, "Yet not what I will, but what you will" (Mark 14:36). And ultimately he became "obedient to the point of death, even death on a cross" (Phil. 2:8). Jesus submitted to the Father.

A wife reflects Jesus when she submits to her husband's initiative. This means she will follow her husband's leading even when she prefers or desires another way. As a godly woman wedded to a man, she will submit to his sacrificial initiative and so reflect the glory of Jesus's submission to the Father. The exception is when the husband's will would lead her into sin. Even then, her resistance is a winsome call to repentance motivated by a broken heart, because she wants her husband to honor the Lord.

Lastly, in her humble submission to her husband's leadership, she will be exalted. Paul tells us that, based on Christ's submission, "God has highly exalted him and bestowed on him the name that is above every name" (Phil. 2:9). God exalted Jesus because he humbly submitted himself to the Father's headship.

God will often exalt the persevering godly wife in this life (see Prov. 31:28–29). And even if not in this life, certainly in the judgment to come she will receive her reward for her submission. And in that final, glorious exaltation, she will reflect Jesus Christ who was exalted for his humble submission.

The husband reflects Jesus's love as he serves and sacrifices for his wife's good. The wife reflects Jesus's love as she humbly and boldly submits to the leading of her husband, looking forward to the exaltation to come.

Marriage is a unique and wonderful stage filled with daily opportunities to reflect the glories of King Jesus.

Talk about It

Discuss sacrificial leadership and glad submission in your marriage. Does this resonate with how you've already understood marriage? If not, what needs to change or be rethought?

3
Serpents, Seeds, and a Savior

NANCY DEMOSS WOLGEMUTH

Now the serpent was more crafty than any other beast of the field that the LORD God had made. He said to the woman, "Did God actually say, 'You shall not eat of any tree in the garden'?"
–Genesis 3:1

I landed in Genesis 3 seven weeks to the day after my recent marriage. We are still very much newlyweds. Very much in love. Still amazed at what God has brought to pass. Still in awe of the gift God has given us in each other. Still enthralled by and exploring the wonder of what it is to be "one flesh."

And already aware of the presence of the serpent in our marriage. An intruder who knows better than most what God intends for our marriage to be—one who despises the One who joined us together and hates the Story our marriage is meant to tell.

This villain, disguised in a cloak of light, posturing as a voice of reason and rightness, comes to me in unguarded moments. He comes to us in the sweet garden of our newfound love and plants in the soil of my mind seeds of doubt about things God has revealed to be true; conjures up fears that my Creator may not have my best interests at heart; beckons me to exalt my will over God's, to imagine that my way is superior to his, and to strike out independently of my God and my groom.

I recognize the serpent's subtle but nefarious influence:

- when being heard and understood matters more to me than listening and being understanding
- when being proven right is of greater concern to me than being humble
- when I assume the best about myself and less than the best about my precious Adam
- when I magnify my husband's shortcomings in my mind, while making allowances for (or being oblivious to) my own
- when I fancy being the kind of wife I have often challenged others to be, apart from a daily, moment-by-moment infusion of his supernatural, enabling grace
- when my needs and plans and priorities feel more pressing to me than those of my husband

- when being seen and known feels scary and confining
- when working at two-becoming-one seems like more effort than I want to give at the moment
- when I try to control my man or the outcome of a conversation or decision
- when I wrest the staff from my shepherd's hands

Genesis 3 reminds me that none of this should come as a surprise—that I am not the first bride to hear and to heed the serpent's siren, that his tactics were first tried on newlyweds, that he aims to separate what God has joined together.

It reminds me that pain and alienation and broken promises are the fruit of trusting the serpent rather than the One who made and married my mate and me.

It also reminds me that no sooner had that first bride succumbed to the serpent's sound than another seed was sown—sown by a God who pursued the wandering woman's heart with infinite mercy and grace, the seed of the gospel, of promises made and kept, promises of a bruised Seed who would one day rise up to crush the serpent's head.

It reminds me that my hope and the well-being of our marriage do not rest in my husband's strength or mine, or in our determined efforts to do this well. Our hope is in that holy Seed, wounded for us, who took our shame as his own, gave himself up for us, and clothed our nakedness with garments of his own righteousness, acquired by the shedding of his blood.

This Savior will enable us to hold fast to one another, to love each other deeply, selflessly, and faithfully, to live as one flesh, to humbly, joyfully fulfill our God-given responsibilities in this marriage, to escape the serpent's entreaties, to walk together in the light with our Maker, to be forgiven when we fall, and to join him in overcoming the serpent's evil designs.

Talk about It

Affirm your spouse for the ways he or she reflects God's good purposes for your marriage. What patterns of joyful obedience do you see? How, by God's grace, have you grown together?

4

A Special Agent
for Change

MARSHALL SEGAL

*God created man in his own image, in the image of God
he created him; male and female he created them. And
God blessed them. And God said to them, "Be fruitful and
multiply and fill the earth." . . . And God saw everything
that he had made, and behold, it was very good.*
—Genesis 1:27–28, 31

There was a day—or at least a few hours—when marriage was pure, undefiled, free from sin and selfishness.
In fact, the whole world was that way. God had looked
on his creation and it was good—complete, flawless, rich,
and filled with life (Gen. 1:31). And a central part of that
truly utopian world was marriage—a man and a woman

joined together as one in a God-ordained, God-filled, and God-glorifying union (Gen. 1:27).

Marriage wasn't an optional, incidental arrangement in God's agenda. It was right there at the center, tying together the two most significant characters in this new and epic story. For sure, sin has broken and marred what was good and pure about that first marriage. But Paul says, quoting Genesis 2, that from the very beginning, the mystery of marriage is that it's meant to represent Jesus's relationship with the church (Eph. 5:31–32). This means sin wasn't a surprise in God's design for marriage. Rather, it tragically, but beautifully, served to fulfill God's good design.

Marriages today, though flawed, are still carrying out, though imperfectly, the glorious purposes God gave them in the garden—purposes like our sanctification. If you put two God-fearing, Jesus-following, but sinful people in such close proximity, with a covenant to keep them from running away, there will be tension, conflict, and *hopefully* change.

Perhaps the greatest means God has given us, under the Holy Spirit, for making us more like himself are the people in our lives who love us enough to confront our patterns of selfishness, unhealthiness, and sin. Marriage places that loving person with us in the same family, the same house, the same budget, and the same covenant promise. If God is unfailingly faithful to his promises, and the Spirit really is more powerful than our weaknesses, and we both truly want more of God, he'll be using us to eradicate sin and cultivate righteousness in one another.

Talk about It

Discuss how sin coming into the world has fundamentally changed the everyday experience of marriage. How would your marriage be different without sin? In God's wise and mysterious plan, what opportunities does the reality of sin present to your marriage?

5

Sex Is for Believers

JOHN PIPER

Everything created by God is good, and nothing is
to be rejected if it is received with thanksgiving, for
it is made holy by the word of God and prayer.
—1 Timothy 4:4–5

God designed the pleasures of sex for the enjoyment of
Christians. We might lose sight of this, since Hollywood
has ripped the curtains off the sacred marriage bed and
turned a luxuriant, holy pleasure into a cheap spectator
sport. We might be tempted to think that, since sex is so
sinfully misused and so universally undermining to the
all-satisfying beauty of Christ's holiness, maybe we Christians should have nothing to do with it.

Paul says the opposite. It is the world that has stolen
what belongs to believers. Sex belongs to Christians. Because sex belongs to God. God created it "to be received

with thanksgiving by those who believe and know the truth" (1 Tim. 4:3).

If it is used by those who do not believe and know the truth, it is prostituted. They have exchanged the glory of God for images (Rom. 1:23). They have torn sex from its God-appointed place in the orbit of marriage. But they do not know what they are doing, and apart from God's intervening, saving grace, the price they will pay in this life and the next is incalculable.

The pleasures of sex are meant for believers. They are designed for their greatest expression by the children of God. He saves his richest gifts for his children. And as we enjoy his gift of sex, we say, by our covenant faithfulness to our spouse, that God is greater than sex. And the pleasures of sex are themselves an overflow of God's own goodness. This pleasure is less than what we will know fully in him at his right hand. And in it, we taste something of his very exquisiteness.

When the preciousness and pleasures of Christ are supreme, all dimensions of sex, including *experiencing* pleasure, *seeking* pleasure, *giving* pleasure, and *abstinence from* pleasure, will all find their biblical and Christ-exalting expression.

Everything God made is good. Everything is for the sake of worship and love. And this is true both in the feasting and the fasting. In the sexual union and in abstinence. Sex is made for the glory of Christ—for the Christ-exalting glory of covenant-keeping faithfulness in marriage, and for the glory of Christ-exalting chastity in singleness. It is always good. Sex is always an occasion to show that the Giver of sex is better than sex.

Talk about It

Discuss the extent to which the world's view of sex has influenced your own. How should knowing that "sex is for believers" affect the way you think and feel about sex?

6

Marital Intimacy Is More Than Sex

JOSH SQUIRES

Above all, keep loving one another earnestly.
—1 Peter 4:8

Usually when husbands and wives begin to feel disconnected from one another, the root issue is intimacy. One of the keys to reconnecting is understanding that intimacy is multi-faceted. In fact, there are at least five different types of intimacy. Only when we keep all five functioning can we have marriages that feel profoundly connected.

1. Spiritual Intimacy

This is the hub from which all other intimacy types emerge. If spiritual intimacy is high, the other types of intimacy will have some natural resiliency. Spiritual intimacy comes from being in God's word together, praying for one another, and worshiping together. The word of God is the nourishment of our souls (Matt. 4:4; Deut. 8:3). When we are on the same spiritual diet, we can expect to grow in similar ways and therefore grow together—not separately.

2. Recreational Intimacy

This bond is created and strengthened by sharing recreational activities, from crosswords to hang-gliding. This sort of intimacy tends to be highest early in the relationship when both spouses are willing to try things outside their comfort zone just to be in each other's presence. As presence becomes more the norm—and as life gets more complicated with jobs, kids, and more—opportunities for recreational activities plummet, and the cost can skyrocket. Nonetheless, God has made us to enjoy life's activities—especially with our spouses (Eccles. 9:9)—and our marriages need the ability to laugh and play together if they are to endure the times of tears and toil.

3. Intellectual Intimacy

Husbands and wives also connect by discussing shared topics of interest, whether casually or seriously. The cord of relationship is reinforced when you exercise mentally with your spouse. Movies, politics, cooking—any subject of shared interest is fair game.

Similar to recreational intimacy, intellectual intimacy tends to be at its highest at the beginning of a relationship. As time passes, husbands and wives often assume they know how their spouse thinks on nearly every issue. While they may often be right, it's the details that matter, and there is almost always some new angle to explore. The rewards are well worth it.

4. Physical Intimacy

This is what "intimacy" means to many people, but the subject here is not just sex. A hug, cuddling on the couch, and holding hands definitely count. In fact, one of the biggest complaints for wives is that the husband can take any physical touch as a sign that she wants sexual intimacy, when sometimes she just needs to cuddle.

Of all the types of intimacy, this one pays the biggest dividends for men. Men typically feel the most connected when physical intimacy (and especially sexual physical intimacy) is highest. This is no surprise, as God instructs man to delight in these activities with his wife (Prov. 5:18–19).

5. Emotional Intimacy

Where intellectual intimacy discusses topics and is usually dominated by thoughts, emotional intimacy discusses experience and is usually dominated by feelings. Because men are typically more limited in their emotional vocabulary and less comfortable with emotionally laden speech than their wives, we can misunderstand our wives when they speak. We imagine she wants an exchange of ideas, when what she really wants is someone to identify with her feelings.

Regardless of any limitations, men are called to shepherd their wives' hearts just as much as women are called to shepherd their husband's sexuality. Emotional intimacy is generally where women feel most connected. There is a reason that the first thing the then-sinless Adam did when he first saw Eve was not get her into bed; instead, he uttered the world's first love poem (Gen. 2:23).

Good Cycles and Bad

When men feel disconnected, they often try to get physical intimacy via the route of recreational intimacy (let's do something fun together and maybe we will end up in bed). When women feel disconnected, they often try to get emotional intimacy via the route of intellectual intimacy (let's talk about something and maybe we will end up sharing our feelings).

Here couples can easily find themselves in cycles of isolation, as they focus more on getting than on giving. This is where the Christian commitment to love one another, even when it hurts (John 13:34–35; Gal. 5:13; 6:2; Eph. 4:2, 32; 1 Pet. 4:8–10), can help the couple move from cycles of isolation to cycles of intimacy as they lovingly put each other's needs before their own.

Pursuing connection with one another helps ground us in the intimate love of the one in whom our connection is eternal and unfailing: God himself.

Talk about It

Do you identify with the typical patterns of pursuing intimacy (men: recreational in pursuit of sexual; women: intellectual in pursuit of emotional)? Discuss ways in which you feel loved, and ask how you can do a better job of communicating love to your spouse.

7

Superior Women— and the Men Who Can't Out-Give Them

DOUGLAS WILSON

An excellent wife is the crown of her husband.
—Proverbs 12:4

Near the end of his classic book *Democracy in America*, Alexis De Tocqueville said this:

> Now that I am drawing to the close of this work, in which I have spoken of so many important things done by the Americans, to what the singular prosperity and growing strength

of that people ought mainly to be attributed, I
should reply: To the superiority of their women.

Now the point in bringing this up is not to make any
claims about the essential nature of Americans, who are
sinners like everybody else, or to get moderns to trip
over the word *superiority*. Rather, the point is a simple
one—during a critical time in our nation's development,
the women had a remarkable impact, and that (given
the times) the potency of their virtue had little to do
with many of the tricks that we use today to "empower
women."

A godly wife does not just adorn herself; she adorns
her husband. She is a crown of glory. She does this as
a virtuous woman, and this is precious, in part, because
of its comparative rarity. If it were easy, more would be
happy to be virtuous. So at the heart of an adorned and
adorning wife is her deep and abiding fear of God.

The Bible describes a woman who is graced with
wisdom and kindness in these terms: "A gracious woman
retaineth honor: and strong men retain riches" (Prov. 11:16,
KJV). Just as riches flow to a strong man, so also honor
flows to a gracious woman. So a woman is the crown and
glory of her husband to the extent that she is a *gracious*
woman. If she is, then she retains honor as one who has
fulfilled her calling.

Doing this, she *completes* her husband: God has said
that it is not good for him to be alone, but also that it
would be better for him to be alone than to have an un-
gracious wife. *A gracious woman completes her husband.*

She reverences her husband, which is not a servile
fear, but rather a wholesome and godly reverence. Anyone

who thinks that this demeans women needs to get out more. She does not honor him the way a serf honors the king, but rather honors him the way a crown honors a king. *A gracious woman honors her husband.*

And living this way, she does good to her husband. As he provides for her, she manages his household well. "She does him good, and not harm, all the days of her life" (Prov. 31:12). *A gracious woman enriches her husband.*

As the quotation from De Tocqueville indicates, when women are virtuous, people notice. Where does this come from? The apostle Paul tells us that a man who loves his wife loves himself (Eph. 5:28).

Godly marriage is designed in such a way as to make it impossible for a man to out-give his wife. This is not because he gets to be the selfish one, but rather this is for the same reason an industrious farmer cannot possibly out-give his field. If a man sacrifices himself for his wife, as Christ did for the church, he will find that she is his thirty, sixty, and one-hundred fold. As his glory, she brings out his strengths.

She is where his strengths are manifested and come back to bless him.

Talk about It

A godly marriage can make it "impossible for a man to out-give his wife." Do you believe this is true? If so, what kinds of sacrifice should that inspire in a husband? And what kind of motivation should that give a wife?

8

Good Listening
Requires Patience

DAVID MATHIS

Let every person be quick to hear, slow to speak, slow to anger.
–James 1:19

Listening is one of the easiest things you'll ever do, and
one of the hardest.

In a sense, listening is easy—or *hearing* is easy. It
doesn't demand the initiative and energy required in
speaking. That's why "faith comes from hearing, and hearing through the word of Christ" (Rom. 10:17). The point
is that hearing is easy, and faith is not an expression of
our activity, but our receiving the activity of another. It is
"hearing with faith" (Gal. 3:2, 5) that accents the achieve-

ments of Christ and thus is the channel of grace that starts and sustains the Christian life.

But despite this ease—or perhaps precisely because of it—we often fight against it. In our sin, we'd rather trust in ourselves than another, amass our own righteousness than receive another's, speak our thoughts rather than listen to someone else. True, sustained, active listening is a great act of faith, and a great means of grace, both for ourselves and our spouse.

The charter text for Christian listening might be James 1:19: "Let every person be quick to hear, slow to speak, slow to anger." It's simple enough in principle, and nearly impossible to live. Too often we are slow to hear, quick to speak, and quick to anger. So learning to listen well won't happen overnight. It requires discipline, effort, and intentionality. You get better with time, they say. Becoming a better listener hangs not on one big resolve to do better in a single conversation, but on developing a pattern of little resolves to focus in on particular people in specific moments.

Dietrich Bonhoeffer, in his book *Life Together*, gives us something to avoid: "a kind of listening with half an ear that presumes already to know what the other person has to say." This, he says, "is an impatient, inattentive listening, that . . . is only waiting for a chance to speak." Perhaps we think we know where our spouse's words are going, and so already begin formulating our response. Or we were in the middle of something when they started talking to us, or have another commitment approaching, and we wish they were done already.

Or maybe we're half-eared because our attention is divided, by our external surroundings or our internal rebounding to self. As Janet Dunn laments, "Unfortunate-ly, many of us are too preoccupied with ourselves when we listen. Instead of concentrating on what is being said, we are busy either deciding what to say in response or men-tally rejecting the other person's point of view."

Positively, then, good listening requires concentration and means we're in with both ears, and that we hear the other person out till they're done speaking. Rarely will the speaker begin with what's most important, and deepest. We need to hear the whole train of thought, all the way to the caboose, before starting across the tracks.

Good listening silences the smartphone and doesn't stop the story, but is attentive and patient. Externally relaxed and internally active. It takes energy to block out the distractions that keep bombarding us, and the peripheral things that keep streaming into our conscious-ness, and the many good possibilities we can spin out for interrupting. When we are people quick to speak, it takes Spirit-powered patience to not only be quick to hear, but to keep on hearing.

Talk about It

Be honest with each other: how are you doing in the min-istry of listening to each other? Begin with yourself. For-mulate together one or two practical steps you can take to show each other more love through engaged listening.

9
We Need to Talk about Submission

KIM CASH TATE

I want you to understand that the head of every man is Christ, the head of a wife is her husband, and the head of Christ is God.
—*1 Corinthians 11:3*

It's surprising today when someone speaks in a straightforward manner of the God-ordained role of a wife to lovingly support and submit to her husband (who has his own God-ordained expectations as he submits to Christ). Increasingly, it seems, the subject is deemed unfit for polite conversation, even among believers—even from the pulpit. Here are three reasons we need to talk unapologetically about submission.

1. Submission Points to the Supremacy of Christ

The husband is the head of his wife *as* Christ is the head of the church. And *as* the church is subject to Christ, so is the wife to her husband, in everything (Eph. 5:22–24). Submission in marriage is but a sub-focus, a reflection. It points to a greater glory.

When we marginalize submission in marriage, we dull the reflection. If we don't talk about it—let alone, live it—the whole notion of submission becomes foreign. The world needs to know that there is divine order and authority. Jesus is King of kings and Lord of lords. He is seated at the right hand of the Father, far above all rule and authority and power and dominion, with everything in subjection under his feet (Eph. 1:20–22). Submission in marriage bears witness to our risen Lord who reigns supreme.

2. Submission Esteems the Truth

As believers, we don't want to resemble in the slightest way those who suppress the truth (Rom. 1:18). To the contrary, our obligation is to uphold the truth of the word of God, no matter the times we live in, no matter how uncomfortable we may be. And granted, we will feel uncomfortable talking about submission in many circles. The discomfort is by design. The god of this world has waged assault on submission in order to suppress this truth.

We would not seek to align ourselves with his mission. Yet, if submission is relegated to the realm of those things we just don't talk about, truth takes a hit. Conversely, when we embrace the beauty and glory in submission and help others to do the same, the word is glorified.

3. Submission Affirms God's Created Order

God fashioned Eve from Adam's rib because Adam needed a suitable helper. Any notion that submission is somehow the product of the fall or of the times in which the New Testament was written is simply untrue. In the garden, where all was declared "very good," submission was in view (Gen. 1:31). It was central to the divine beauty and perfection that existed in their marital relationship.

To retreat from the topic of submission is to throw aside fundamentals of marriage that God ordained from the beginning. If ever there were a time to dialogue about marriage, submission, and the attendant glory of Christ, it is now.

Talk about It

What does submission mean (and not mean) in light of what God, not modern society, has to say? In what specific ways do you feel the rub in your marriage between the contrasting voices of God's word and secular media?

10

As Long as Both Shall Live

What God has joined together, let not man separate.
—Matthew 19:6

On June 29, 2007, my wife and I stood before our pastor, our friends, and our family—and most importantly, before our God—and vowed to each other,

> I will be faithful to you
> In plenty and in want,
> In joy and in sorrow,
> In sickness and in health,
> To love and to cherish,
> As long as we both shall live.

As long as we both shall live. No exceptions. No out-clauses. Not just in plenty, joy, and health, but also in want, sorrow, and sickness. No allowances for any seven-year itches or any other excuse. We left father and mother, covenanted to become one flesh (Gen. 2:24), and have taken Jesus's words with utter seriousness, "What God has joined together, let not man separate" (Matt. 19:6). Neither of us would say that marriage has been easy, but we can say it's glorious that there are no outs but death.

The stresses, strains, tensions, and pains of marriage caught both of us off guard early on. Our dating was so peaceful—too peaceful, it turned out—and engagement only had a few speed bumps. But once we were both all in, both fully believing this was our unbending commitment till death, with no loopholes or exegetical outs, then, with the conditionality of dating and engagement aside, and the unconditionality of covenantal marriage now in place, we were finally free to be our real selves. Which was such a good thing, though it soon got a little messy.

But these were good messes to make, ones we desperately needed (and still need). All along the mess had been inside us (and still is), in our selfish and sinful hearts, and the real cleaning couldn't begin happening until it was out in the open. We both previously had Christian roommates and disciplers who had pressed on our own sin and pushed us toward Jesus. But something about this lifelong covenant—something about knowing that the gig with this one roommate is till death do us part—forced us to speak up about the quirks, idiosyncrasies, and sins we otherwise could have ignored for a few months or a couple years.

As two rescued sinners, banking on Jesus for eternal redemption and for increasing redemption here in this life, we didn't want to keep everything at surface level. We wanted to truly know each other, and become our true selves in Christ, not just the best face we could put on before marriage. We could have tried living on and on with a façade of harmony, and never strained to go deeper, and experienced only the thin joy that comes from keeping everything at the surface. But we wanted more (we still want more). We wanted greater joy. We wanted fuller satisfaction. We wanted the greater pleasure that comes only on the other side of pain and difficulty. We wanted the better relationship that comes only after things first get worse. And marriage with no exits but death has forced the issue.

But not only is "as long as we both shall live" better for us and for our children (much could be said about that), but we're better able to witness to the world. The world is full of relationships with strings attached. In some of those, like employment, conditions are good and necessary. But when every relationship is fraught with conditions, it can feel like there's no rest for the weary.

The world needs to see in Christian marriages a pointer to the Savior who, without conditions, chose to set his love on his bride, the church (Eph. 1:4–6), and through thick and thin, with all her failures and unfaithfulnesses, continues working to "sanctify her, having cleansed her by the washing of water with the word, so that he might present the church to himself in splendor, without spot or wrinkle or any such thing, that she might be holy and without blemish" (Eph. 5:26–27).

When the exceptions and conditions are gone at the
most fundamental level, a man must learn to "love his
wife as himself" (Eph. 5:33) and discover the joy of Acts
20:35: "It is more blessed to give than to receive." In the
covenant, we can no more leave behind the reality of our
marriage than we can abandon our own bodies. "Husbands should love their wives as their own bodies" (Eph.
5:28).

Talk about It

Find a copy of your wedding vows, and read them together. Discuss what difference it makes to have committed
yourself to each other in good times and bad, sickness and
health, for richer or for poorer, with no outs but death
itself. How does marriage without conditions make your
relationship stronger, not weaker?

11

Unembarrassed by the Bible

JOHN PIPER

Let your fountain be blessed, and rejoice in the wife of your youth, a lovely deer, a graceful doe. Let her breasts fill you at all times with delight; be intoxicated always in her love. Why should you be intoxicated, my son, with a forbidden woman and embrace the bosom of an adulteress? For a man's ways are before the eyes of the LORD, and he ponders all his paths.
—Proverbs 5:18–21

We are not supposed to be embarrassed by the forthright sensuality of sexual love in marriage as the Bible portrays it—sometimes graphically.

It is no shame that "a man's ways are before the Lord" as her breasts fill him at all times with delight.

This is why God made her that way and him that way. In fact, that this delight in her is "before" the Lord—in the presence of the Lord—points to the truth that all our joy in what God has made is meant to be a delight in God. There is something of his glory in all the glories of the world.

We are not meant to revel in his creation *instead of* him or *more than* in him but because of him, and because there is something of him in all that is good and beautiful. The heavens are telling the glory of God (Ps. 19:1). We are to see it. And worship him. So it is with the breasts of our wives. The breasts are telling the glory of God, the goodness of God, the beauty of God, and more. We are to see it. And worship him.

The Song of Solomon is in the Bible, among other reasons, to make sure that we take seriously the exquisite physical pleasures between a bride and a groom as a picture of Christ and his church. The point is not that we nullify the physical pleasures of this Song by seeing it as a full-color image of Ephesians 5:22–33. The point is that we let the Song stun us that God would design such a relationship between man and woman—from the beginning—as the image of the covenant-keeping pleasures between Christ and his church.

Talk about It

Read aloud Song of Solomon 4:5–7 and 7:3–10, and answer together these two questions: 1) What is the significance for our marriage that marital love and sex are celebrated like this in God's holy word? 2) What makes me most uneasy with such a view of marital love, and why might it be that I feel this way?

12

Do You Expect Your Marriage to Be Easy?

ADRIEN SEGAL

God shows his love for us in that while we
were still sinners, Christ died for us.
—Romans 5:8

When we get married, most of us believe deep down that while lots of marriages are really hard, ours will be different. Sure, there may be hard things here and there, but when we lock arms with our soul mate, the mountains will melt under our feet.

Adam seemed to feel this way—and it's understandable before the entrance of sin into the world. When he first saw the woman God had created to be his companion, he could not contain his joy: "This at last is bone of my bones and flesh of my flesh" (Gen. 2:23). Somewhere deep inside, Adam appreciated that the woman, being formed by God from Adam's own flesh to be his helper, would meet needs of companionship, support, and pleasure like nothing else God had created. And she would, for God saw that it was "not good that the man should be alone" (Gen. 2:18), and in his compassion, God created the perfect mate for Adam.

Adam's expectations were as high as they could be on that first day, for he had not yet been corrupted by sin and seen its consequences. But his understandable, even righteous, naiveté did not keep him from the harsh realities to come. The pretty picture of friendship and intimacy tragically and violently falls apart in Genesis 3.

Did God make a mistake? Did he not see that this woman's weakness in judgment would lead mankind into destruction? Did he not see that the marriage between Adam and Eve would be harder than they could have ever imagined? They literally gave up paradise to struggle for every mouthful of food.

No marriage has ever been easy. The amazing thing is that we always seem to expect it will be for us.

Love in a Land of Easy

Of course, marriage is not the problem. Sin is the problem. Sin makes every marriage hard.

Apparently, then, God didn't create marriage to make life easy. He created it to unfold beauty, depth, strength, and love that could never be discovered in a land of "easy." God created marriage to help us know what real love looks like.

The Best Marriage and Worst Bride

We, the church, have the unspeakable privilege of being the bride of Christ (Eph. 5:25; Rev. 19:7–9). In this marriage, we see love like Hosea's—lavishly poured on the bride by her groom, even when she scorns him, reviles him, and seeks her pleasure in others (Hos. 2:14–23). We see a love that never gives up, no matter how often the bride runs to lesser gods to seek joy that can only be found in the true Bridegroom (Rom. 8:38–39). We see that Groom's breathtaking, unexplainable sacrificial love unto death in order to keep and preserve a bride—a bride who daily seems to consider that gift less important than the comparatively insignificant earthly needs she expects him to fill today (Rom. 5:8; Isa. 53:1–12).

This is not a pretty picture. But paradoxically, it is a stunningly beautiful one. The harder God is willing to fight to demonstrate his love, the more beautiful it becomes.

Why God Gave You Marriage

Marriage—and all very hard things we experience in this life—are a means God has devised to help us drink deeply of the immeasurable glory of genuine love. We would never see this beauty and depth strolling down an easy road. Persistent, striving, overcoming effort fueled by the sustaining power of our Creator God ultimately yields deep joy and satisfaction that selfish, spoiling, "easy" love would never experience or display. The best picture we have of this is the cross. Praise God that Jesus didn't expect his marriage to his bride to be easy. But because he was faithful in the hardest, ugliest marriage ever, we may now enjoy pleasures forevermore.

In marriage, God calls you to display the love that God has shown you to the precious person made in his image that he has joined you to. God hasn't encouraged you to seek all your satisfaction from your spouse—only God can be the source of your satisfaction. But God has called you to show your spouse and others what *God's* love looks like. Not love between sinless people, but grace-filled, patient, and forgiving love. Love like Christ's. What a high and holy calling. Husbands and wives who understand this will find that the hardest things they endure together are indeed some of the most beautiful and sanctifying.

Talk about It

Do you believe your marriage will "be different," that others may have difficulty, but yours will be easy? Talk honestly about how your marriage is proving different than you expected.

13

The Call to Love and Respect

DOUGLAS WILSON

Husbands, love your wives, as Christ loved the church and gave himself up for her . . . and let the wife see that she respects her husband.
–Ephesians 5:25, 33

Scripture teaches us that Christians should honor or respect all men (1 Pet. 2:17). Every human being bears the image of God, and so, of course, we are called on to respect and honor that. And of course, Scripture also teaches us to love our neighbor (Lev. 19:18), and Jesus in his famous story makes the point that our neighbor is whatever person God has placed right in front of us (Luke

10:29–37). So all Christians are to love everyone, and all
Christians should honor everyone. That is the baseline.

But when we come down to the particular relationship of husbands to wives, and wives to husbands, Scripture gives us an important, additional emphasis. Husbands
are told specifically to love their wives as Christ loved the
church (Eph. 5:25). Wives are told specifically to respect
their husbands as the church does Christ (Eph. 5:33).

These commands are directed to our respective and
relative weaknesses. We are told to do things that we
might not do unless we were told. For example, children
are told to obey their parents because it is easy for children not to do so (Eph. 6:1). In the same way, husbands
are told to love their wives because it is easy for husbands
not to do so. Wives are told to honor their husbands
because it is easy for wives not to do so. We are called to
do things that might not occur to us. If we were all doing
these things naturally, why bring it up?

Women are better at loving than men are. Men do
well at respecting. C. S. Lewis once observed that women
think of love as taking trouble for others—which is much
closer to a scriptural *agape* love than what men naturally
do. Men tend to think of love as not giving trouble to
others.

So men must be *called* to sacrifice for their wives,
to take trouble for them, as Christ gave himself for the
church. Women must be urged to respect their husbands.
A woman can naturally love a man she does not honor
or respect very much, and this is something that Paul
would identify as a trouble. How many times have we
heard a terrible story about a girl returning to her abusive
boyfriend because she "loves him," even though he treats

her like dirt? But if we asked her if she respects him, she would reply, "Are you kidding? *Him*?" And men must be called to give themselves away for their wives. This is what a wedding means.

Talk about It

Discuss whether these distinct emphases for wives to be loved, and husbands to be respected, fits with your own experience and knowledge of your heart. How can this insight help you in learning to love/respect your spouse well?

14

Love Is More
Than a Choice

JOHN PIPER

*Let all bitterness and wrath and anger and clamor
and slander be put away from you, along with all
malice. Be kind to one another, tenderhearted, forgiving
one another, as God in Christ forgave you.*
—Ephesians 4:31–32

This is a gentle pushback on a popular saying.

There is truth in saying "love is a choice" or "love is a decision." It is true that if you don't feel like doing good to your neighbor, love will incline you to "choose" to do it anyway. If you feel like getting a divorce, love will incline you to "choose" to stay married and work it out.

If you shrink back from the pain of nails being driven through your hands, love will incline you to say, "Not my will, but yours, be done" (Luke 22:42). That's the *truth* I hear in the statements "love is a choice" or "love is a decision."

But I don't *prefer* to use these statements. Too many people hear three tendencies in them that those who use the statements may not intend.

1. Saying "love is a choice" sounds like the tendency to believe love is in our power to perform, even when we don't feel like it.
2. Saying "love is a choice" sounds like the tendency to make the will, with its decisions, the decisive moral agent rather than the heart, with its affections.
3. Saying "love is a choice" sounds like the tendency to set the bar too low: If you can will to treat someone well, you have done all you should.

I disagree with all three of these tendencies. In their place I would say this: Both at the level of desiring to do good, and the level of willing the good we don't desire, we are totally dependent on the decisive grace of God. All that honors Christ—both affections and choices—are gifts to fallen sinners (1 Cor. 4:7; Gal. 5:22–23).

Beneath the will, with its decisions, there is the heart, which produces our preferences, and these preferences guide the will. "The good person out of the good treasure of his heart produces good, and the evil person out of his evil treasure produces evil, for out of the abundance of the heart his mouth speaks" (Luke 6:45).

If our love is only a choice, it is not yet what it ought to be.

It is important to hear me say "*more* than a decision." I am not denying there are crucial choices and decisions to be made in a life of love. I am not denying that those choices and decisions are part of what love *is*. So I am not saying the statements "love *is* a choice" or "love *is* a decision" are false.

But I am jealous that the richness and depth (and human impossibility) of what love is in the Bible not be lost. Hence this little pushback.

Talk about It

In your marriage, how might you be compromising your own long-term joy if you only thought of love as a choice or decision? On the other side, how might it be detrimental to your marriage if you only thought of love as a feeling, and not also a decision? In what concrete ways can you make your love for one another more than just a decision?

15

Wedded in a Real War

FRANCIS CHAN

Though we walk in the flesh, we are not waging war according to the flesh. For the weapons of our warfare are not of the flesh but have divine power to destroy strongholds.
—2 Corinthians 10:3–4

The Bible teaches that we are in a real war with a real enemy (2 Cor. 10:3–4; Eph. 6:10–20).

God has given us a mission, so we cannot allow ourselves to get "entangled in civilian pursuits" (2 Tim. 2:4). Picture a nice house with a white picket fence and your happy family lounging inside. Now imagine a full-scale war unfolding just a few blocks away. Your friends and neighbors are fighting for their lives while you are remodeling your kitchen and hanging your new big-screen TV. You have contractors installing better windows so you can tune out all of the noise.

It is a pretty pathetic picture, but it's an appropriate comparison for the lives that are offered to so many Christian couples. They are ignoring Jesus's mission in hopes of enjoying this life. But don't fall for it. Real life is found in the battle. Right now, we have many brothers and sisters being tortured overseas because of their faith. Let's pray for them and be encouraged by their example to enter the fight.

Being in war together may be what keeps us from being at war with each other. Rather than neglecting the battle to work on your marriage, maybe the best thing for your marriage is to enter the battlefield together.

Talk about It

Are you part of God's global mission together as a couple? How can your marriage participate practically in the spiritual struggle for the souls of humanity, rather than tuning out what's really going on in the world, while trying to build your own façade of heaven here?

16

Five Things Submission Does Not Mean

Likewise, wives, be subject to your own husbands, so that even if some do not obey the word, they may be won without a word by the conduct of their wives, when they see your respectful and pure conduct.
—1 Peter 3:1

1. Submission Does Not Mean You Always Accept Your Husband's Perspective

The text encompasses marriages in which the wife is a Christian and the husband is not. So if that wife can't be humbly submissive to her husband without accepting his view of Jesus, the text doesn't make sense. And if a wife can disagree on this supreme issue and still be submissive, in a Christian marriage the wife can humbly disagree with her husband on lesser issues.

My wife would tell you, "We settled the principle early that if we can't agree, Johnny's going to make the call." That's really basic. And we almost never get to that point. One reason is that I often yield to her, "You were right; I was wrong." A husband's leadership does not mean he doesn't listen, or that he always gets the last word. God has made the wife with a mind. She is a person, not a body and not a machine.

2. Submission Does Not Mean You Never Try to Influence Your Husband

The whole point of the text is to "win him." Her *life* is devoted to helping this husband change from an unbeliever to a believer. Again, this clearly allows for a wife trying to help her husband grow spiritually within a Christian marriage. If he needs that, then she wants to win him over, to help him see he needs to change. She wouldn't be a loving person if she didn't. So she seeks to help him. That may sound insubordinate to some. Biblically, it isn't.

3. Submission Does Not Mean You Put the Will of Your Husband Before the Will of Christ

Christ is Lord of the believing wife, so *for the Lord's sake* she will submit to the man who *is* her husband but is *not* her Lord. Wherever she must choose between the two, she chooses Jesus. If her husband says, "Let's get involved in a scam," or, "Let's have group sex," her choice is clear. She goes with Jesus on this. She would say it not with a haughty or arrogant attitude, but rather with a winsome, submissive, longing one. He will be able to discern in her a longing that he not do this thing *so that* she could enjoy him as her leader. Do you feel that? "I will not follow your lead on this, and I am *not* following you with a demeanor that tells you I *want* to follow your leadership but cannot in this moment, in this way."

4. Submission Does Not Mean You Get All Your Spiritual Strength Through Your Husband

In the text, the wife has lots of spiritual strength, but none of it is coming through her unbelieving husband. Her hope is in *God*. She's probably going to church on Sunday morning before he gets up, getting her strength elsewhere, getting her worldview elsewhere. If her husband *is* a Christian, and therefore a special channel of God's grace to her, she will get some of her spiritual strength through him. But since her husband is not her Lord, much of her spiritual strength will still come from elsewhere: the Spirit of God, the Word of God, and the people of God.

5. Submission Does Not Mean You Live or Act in Fear

This God-fearing wife is fearless, even in the face of things that are objectively frightening. How much more fearless can she be when her husband is also a believer?

Therefore, in light of everything I have said submission is *not*, I would define submission in marriage like this: *Submission is the defined calling of a wife to honor and affirm her husband's leadership, and so help to carry it through according to her gifts.*

Talk about It

What wrong conceptions have you had (or overheard from others) about "submission" in marriage? Are there any current patterns or practices in your marriage that should change in light of what real submission is and is not?

17

A Possible Marriage-Saver in Nine Steps

JOHN PIPER

Bear with one another and, if one has a complaint against another, forgive each other.
—Colossians 3:13

The grace of God is patient and works both instantaneously and over time. In marriage, a mistake we sometimes make is thinking too idealistically, as though if we blow our first apology, there is no chance for a second.

The way to think about this marriage-saver biblically is that it is an effort to see Colossians 3:13 fleshed out in real life: "Bear with one another and, if one has a complaint against another, forgive each other." There is both "bearing with" and there is "forgiving." How do they mingle in marriage?

Here's one way I have in mind. I will describe nine steps to reconciliation with your wife (or husband, or friend, or colleague). Something like this is needed when you are too sinful to apologize sincerely the first time. This is my real experience more often than I would like to admit, and, in another sense, not often enough. (Wives and husbands, hear these steps with yourself in both roles.)

STEP 1. Your wife points out something you said or did that is wrong or that she doesn't like.

STEP 2. You get angry (for several reasons that seem good to you at the moment).

STEP 3. You have the grace to know in your head that this anger is ungodly and that a heartfelt apology, both for what she pointed out and for the anger, is in order.

STEP 4. You are able to say the words of apology but not able to feel sorry because the anger has made your heart hard toward her. You don't feel tender, you don't feel broken, you don't feel sorry. But you know you should, so you say, "I'm sorry." This is better than silence. It is a partial grace.

STEP 5. She feels that you are angry and is, understandably, not satisfied with words that do not carry heartfelt contrition.

STEP 6. Time goes by. Perhaps an hour or even 24 hours? Two days? The Holy Spirit, ever patient, and relentlessly holy, will not let you go. He works against the anger (James 1:19–20). He stirs up gospel truths (Eph. 4:32). He softens the heart (Ezek. 36:26). This may be through Bible reading, the word of a friend, reading a book, attending a worship service. Meanwhile she is waiting, wondering, praying, hoping.

STEP 7. Anger subsides. Sweetness rises. Tenderness is awakened. Sorrow for sin grows.

STEP 8. You take her aside and you tell her that the first apology was the best you could do at the time because of your sin. You admit it was insufficient. You tell her with tenderness how you feel toward her, and you apologize with heart, and ask for forgiveness.

STEP 9. In mercy, she forgives and things are better.

What I hope you do with this is talk it over with your spouse to see if it fits your experience. One of the values of building this possible pattern into your set of expectations is that you can cut each other some slack (called mercy), so that step 6 doesn't feel hopeless for either partner.

Talk about It

Discuss whether this fits your experience. How can you build a pattern of forgiveness and reconciliation into your marriage?

18

Seven Questions to Ask before Watching Something with Nudity

JOHN PIPER

Blessed are the pure in heart, for they shall see God.
—Matthew 5:8

1. When Will I Tear Out My Eye, If Not Now?

Jesus said everyone who looks at a woman with lustful intent has already committed adultery with her in his heart. If your right eye causes you to sin, tear it out and throw it away (Matt. 5:28–29). Seeing naked women on the screen—or naked men—causes a man, or woman, to sin with their minds and their desires, and often with their bodies. If Jesus told us to guard our hearts by gouging out

our eyes to prevent lust, how much more would he say,
"Don't watch it!"

2. Am I Longing to See God?

I want to see and know God as fully as possible in this life
and the next. Watching nudity is a huge hindrance to that
pursuit. "Blessed are the pure in heart, for they shall see
God" (Matt. 5:8). The defilement of the mind and heart by
watching nudity dulls the heart's ability to see and enjoy
God. I dare anyone to watch nudity and turn straight to
God and give him thanks and enjoy him more because of
what you just experienced.

3. Do I Care about the Souls of the Nudes?

God calls women to adorn themselves in respectable
apparel with modesty and self-control (1 Tim. 2:9). When
we pursue or receive or embrace nudity in our entertain-
ment, we are implicitly endorsing the sin of the women
who sell themselves to this way; we are, therefore, uncar-
ing about their souls. They disobey 1 Timothy 2:9, and if
we watch, we say that's okay.

4. Would I Be Glad If My Daughter Played This Role?

Most Christians are hypocrites in watching nudity because, on the one hand, they say by their watching that
this is okay, and on the other hand, they know deep down
they would not want their daughter or their wife or their
girlfriend to be playing this role. That is hypocrisy.

5. Am I Assuming Nudity Can Be Faked?

Nudity is not like murder and violence on the screen. Violence on a screen is make-believe; nobody really gets killed. But nudity is not make-believe. These actresses are really naked in front of the camera, doing exactly what the director says to do with their legs and their hands and their breasts. And now they are naked in front of millions of people.

6. Am I Assuming Nudity Is Necessary for Good Art?

There is no great film or television series that needs nudity to add to its greatness. No. There isn't. There are creative ways to be true to reality without turning sex into a spectator sport and without putting actors and actresses in morally compromised situations on the set.

It is not artistic integrity that is driving nudity on the screen. Underneath all of this is male sexual appetite driving this business, and following from that is peer pressure in the industry and the desire for ratings that sell. It is not art that puts nudity in film; it's the appeal of prurience. It sells.

7. Am I Free from Doubt?

There is one biblical guideline that makes life very simple: "Whoever has doubts is condemned if he eats, because the eating is not from faith. For whatever does not pro-ceed from faith is sin" (Rom. 14:23). My paraphrase: If you doubt, don't. That would alter the viewing habits of millions, and oh how sweetly they would sleep with their conscience.

So join me; join me in the pursuit of the kind of purity that sees God, and knows the fullness of joy in his presence, and the everlasting pleasure at his right hand (Ps. 16:11).

Talk about It

Discuss your television and movie habits and what it will mean to together embrace Jesus's promise, "Blessed are the pure in heart." Are there any shows or movies you have watched recently that have jeopardized your purity of heart? If so, what can you learn from this to make wiser choices in the future?

19

Do Not Deprive
One Another

JOHN PIPER

*Do not deprive one another, except perhaps by agreement
for a limited time, that you may devote yourselves to
prayer; but then come together again, so that Satan may
not tempt you because of your lack of self-control.
—1 Corinthians 7:5*

God made sexual relations to be profoundly mutual in
marriage; each gives, each receives, each feels the act as
the consummation of a wider and deeper spiritual and
personal union for which sex is only one of the cap-
stones—but an important one. Each spouse is saying, "To
you, and you only, do I give in this way. From you, and
from you only, do I receive in this way."

But couples seldom have the same level of interest and passion about sexual relations. And that relates to frequency, location, timing, methods, privacy, and kinds of touch. No couple has the same comfort level with all these variables. Therefore, how do we live together sexually when desires in all (or some) of these areas are significantly different?

The key passage of Scripture where Paul addresses this directly is 1 Corinthians 7:3–5. The most obvious point in this passage is that Paul commends relatively frequent sexual relations: "Do not deprive one another, except perhaps by agreement *for a limited time* . . . but then come together again, so that Satan may not tempt you."

What is less obvious: Whose desires should govern *how* this act of sex happens?

Paul says, "Wife, accede to your husband's desires." And he says, "Husband, accede to your wife's desires." "For the wife does not have authority over her own body, but the husband does. Likewise the husband does not have authority over his own body, but the wife does" (1 Cor. 7:4). So *she* gets to call the shots—and *he* gets to call the shots.

Now what do you do if the shots are not the same?

I don't think Paul slipped up here and contradicted himself. Paul is not that kind of person, and he is guided by the Holy Spirit. I think he knew exactly what he was doing. He knew that he was dealing with one of the deepest, most complex, emotional moments in human life. Any simple formula will not fit reality for who gets to do what and when and where and how.

The reality is that in a Christian marriage, where the couple is growing in grace, they will figure this out along the lines of Romans 12:10: "Outdo one another in show-ing honor"—or outdo one another in showing grace or mercy or love or kindness or gentleness. This is the most wonderful kind of competition.

She will want to honor him by giving him what he desires. And he will want to honor her by giving her what she desires, which may be less of his desire. And they will pray, and they will talk, and they will struggle, and they will grow along the way.

Talk about It

Take a few moments now (and schedule more time for later if needed) to discuss your desires for sex related to frequency, location, timing, methods, privacy, kinds of touch, and any other relevant aspects. Discover at least one way, if not several, that you can grow in trying to out-do one another in showing honor. (Engaged couples, you can skip this discussion for now!)

20

The Single Key to Personal Change

JOHN PIPER

*A man shall leave his father and mother and hold
fast to his wife, and the two shall become one
flesh." This mystery is profound, and I am saying
that it refers to Christ and the church.
—Ephesians 5:31–32*

I believe that the main way the Bible works (and the main way that preaching works when it is faithful to the Bible) is not to focus us on application. Application is good and right and needful, and nitty-gritty examples and illustrations can be helpful. But I believe that the main way the Bible works is to display glories.

And here is a profound glory: marriage, in its deepest meaning, is a copy of Christ and his church. If you want to understand God's meaning for marriage, if you want to see marriage in its highest possible glory, you have to grasp that we are dealing with a copy.

Marriage isn't an end in itself. This is why marriage doesn't exist in the resurrection (Matt. 22:30). It is a copy. Copies aren't needed anymore when the reality is on full display. Here they are needed. The world is filled with the need for this very kind of marriage. But it won't be needed in the end.

That's because marriage is a copy of a greater original, a metaphor of a greater reality, a parable of a greater truth. And that original, that reality, that truth is God's marriage to his people—Christ's marriage to his church.

We are designed and made to know that which we don't yet know. Why don't we know? Because our hearts and minds are so often consumed with the worthless things of this world. But by the Holy Spirit, in a moment of illumination, all of that can just be driven out, and something absolutely glorious enters into a human heart and changes everything by virtue of its magnitude.

Before any application ever arrives, you are just changed. Suddenly a husband's heart soars with a new sense of what he is on the planet for, and what this woman in her magisterial dignity as his bride is really all about. Everything changes when something lands on you like that with biblical force.

I can have a little misgiving when a husband's response to hearing about the glories of marriage is, "Yeah, but give me an example." All right. I will give an example. But is your heart exploding with this truth? Are you soaring? From those new heights she looks different, the kids look different, the job looks different, the planet looks different, life looks different, death looks different, the devil looks different.

Again, marriage in its deepest possible meaning, in its most profound glory, is a copy of Christ and his church. Marvel at that. Be in awe. It is wonder that changes people, not examples. Examples and illustrations and action lists are a little bit helpful, but seeing glory changes everything.

Talk about It

Pray together now, taking turns, reveling in the wonder of God's grace to us in his Son, that he would take the church as his bride. Praise God together that you get to display that glory in the everyday life of marriage.

21

Budgeting to Bless Your Spouse

MARSHALL SEGAL

The love of money is a root of all kinds of evils. It is through this craving that some have wandered away from the faith and pierced themselves with many pangs.
—1 Timothy 6:10

Because of what the Bible warns about wealth, Christians quickly become some of the most vigilant about their incomes, investments, and donations—and that is a good and right trend as a whole.

There is a brand of budgeting, though, that wears the heroic cape of Christianity, while masking a secret infatuation with money. A lust for more and more money to buy more and more things is evil, and it ironically and tragically steals and murders the life and happiness it promises. A love for money *can* look like a love to have or a love to spend. A love for money might also reveal itself in an obsession with saving or *even* giving money away.

Christian, have you fallen in love with the money you refuse to spend?

One way this kind of frugality can eat away at us is by keeping us from blessing the ones close to us—friends, neighbors, even our own families. There's a thriftiness that will erode important relationships over time. The same safeguards that guard us from spending on selfish, temporary comforts for ourselves can often prevent us from good, tangible acts of love toward others in our lives.

The reasonable logic might say we wouldn't buy that for ourselves, so we shouldn't buy it for others. Or maybe we think of it in terms of need. They don't really *need* that, so I'm not going to get it for them. I'll wait until they actually need something to live. At our worst, we're so focused on our own needs and plans that we just miss the opportunity altogether.

While wisdom prioritizes need and stays within its limits, generosity gladly spends on others, even when it wouldn't spend on itself. God has given us a responsibility to model his sacrificial, generous, even lavish love for people in our lives, especially our families. Just like in his provision for us, this will often mean purchasing something special, unexpected, even unneeded in order to express our love for and commitment to others.

Talk about It

Take a few moments to talk about finances in view of the biblical truth that money is for helping people hope in God. What is your tendency as a couple? Are you so tight with money that it threatens to compromise your love for others?

22

A Wife's Responsibility in Solving Marital Conflict

JOHN PIPER

Wives, be subject to your own husbands, so that
even if some do not obey the word, they may be won
without a word by the conduct of their wives.
–1 Peter 3:1

What is a wife's responsibility in solving marital conflict? It's an interesting question when we consider marriage as a model of Christ and the church—the husband representing Christ, the wife representing the church. We don't want to extend the analogy too far, but it's plain in Scripture, so we should explore it and try to learn from it.

Christ is sovereign, and he takes initiatives. A key initiative is that he puts it in the heart of his church to do

things, especially to pray. So I'm part of the bride. I see a
problem in the relationship between me and Christ. What
should I do? Blame him? I should go to him, talk to him,
ask him for help.

Now a wife is under the Lord Jesus directly for
herself, not just through her husband. So she probably
sees things her husband doesn't, and has unique sensitiv-
ities about what's causing problems in the marriage. So
she should say to God first, "O God, heal this marriage.
Please work on this marriage." And then she should ask,
"Please, give me wisdom how I can help my husband see
what I see." There's a way to be a submissive wife and at
the same time be way ahead of your husband spiritually,
or in a given situation to be much more perceptive than
he is.

On the husband's side, leadership in a marriage
obviously doesn't imply perfection or infallibility, or that
in every situation he knows what's best. But generally he's
taking the initiatives. This means, among other things,
that he's going to care a lot about making his wife full
in her experience of Christ, including her responsibility to point out to him things in his humanity (not his
Christ-likeness) that he's not seeing.

So, yes, we husbands need to hear from our wives
about things we're blind to. But she doesn't want to take
over at that point. She wants to say, "Here's the way I see
it. I think we need to do this or this or this." And then his
job as the leader—and this is *the hardest job* as the leader—is to humble himself to act on that instead of saying,
"Okay, if you don't like the way I do it, go ahead." The
hardest thing in the world can be to receive from your
wife news that you don't want to receive, and then to rise

above the self-pity, the anger, and the frustration of that moment.

So I would say a wife's role is to see all that God enables her to see and then ask him for wise and humble and submissive ways to share, to bring into her husband's life her perspective on things. And it's the husband's job as a leader to be humbly receptive to those kinds of things and then to take action.

Talk about It

Does today's reading bring to mind any recent scenarios in your marriage? Were you able to observe, speak, hear, or act with grace about a point of tension between you? How do you want to handle potential conflict in the future to love and honor your spouse?

23

Men Run on Respect, Women on Love

DOUGLAS WILSON

Husbands, love your wives, as Christ loved the church and gave himself up for her . . . and let the wife see that she respects her husband.
—Ephesians 5:25, 33

The commands to husbands and wives in Ephesians 5 reveal something about the needs of the recipient. In other words, if the Bible said that shepherds should feed the sheep, a reasonable inference would be that sheep need food. When husbands are told to love their wives, we can infer from this that wives need to be loved. When wives are told to respect their husbands, we can infer from this that husbands need to be respected. Think of it as two kinds of car that run on different kinds of fuel—diesel and regular, say. Men run on respect, and wives run on love.

In saying this, remember that we are talking about *emphasis*. On a basic level, everyone needs to be loved and everyone needs to be respected. But when Scripture singles out husbands and wives living together, the men are told to love and the women are told to respect. Flip this around, and you see that men should remember that their wives need to be loved, and their wives should remember that their husbands need to be respected.

Remembering this keeps us from giving what we would like to be getting. I once knew a husband who got his wife a nice shotgun for Christmas. She was a shrewd Christian woman, and so the following Christmas, she got him a nice string of pearls. And as she told my wife, "They were *very* nice pearls."

Often when a marriage is in a tough spot, both spouses tend to give what they feel they need—love and respect, respectively. Wives reach out to their husbands with love, when respect is what would really help. Husbands can back away, thinking of this as a form of respect, "giving space," when what they need to do is close in with love.

Now—here is where it gets glorious—love and respect are both *potent*. The Bible teaches that this kind of love is efficacious. This kind of respect is powerful. This sort of love bestows loveliness. This kind of respect bestows respectability.

Husbands cannot duplicate the love of Christ, which efficaciously made his bride lovely. While we were yet sinners, Christ died for us (Rom. 5:8). But while we cannot duplicate this kind of love, husbands are told to imitate it. And in imitating it, we see some of the comparable effects. A woman who is loved by her husband is a woman who will grow in loveliness. He washes her with the water of God's word (Eph. 5:26). The entire passage assumes that this kind of love bestows loveliness. And the same kind of potency can be found in a godly woman's respect. Peter tells us that reverent and chaste behavior can break down a man's disobedient spirit (1 Pet. 3:1–2).

So then, men and women should love and respect each other. They should do so with all their hearts. But when they are concentrating on their marriages, the men should lean into love. The women should lean into respect. The results can be astonishing.

Talk about It

Think back in your relationship about an instance, perhaps even this week, when you sought to give your spouse what you wanted to get, rather than what they needed to receive. Talk through the details with your spouse, and plan ahead for how you might do better. Specifically, how can a husband help make his wife more lovable by loving her? How can a wife help make her husband more worthy of respect by respecting him?

24

Just Forgive and Forbear?

JOHN PIPER

If anyone is caught in any transgression, you who are
spiritual should restore him in a spirit of gentleness.
—Galatians 6:1

Marriage should not be—and God willing, need not
be—a static stretch of time inhabited by changeless
personalities in durable conflict. Even that is better than
divorce in God's eyes, and has a glory of its own. But it is
not the best picture of Christ and the church.

So God gives grace not only to forgive and to for-
bear, but also to be transformed so that less forgiving and
forbearing are needed. Grace is not just power to return

good for evil, but also power to do less evil. Even power to be less bothersome.

And sometimes, in order to be transformed, we need to be confronted.

In Christ's relationship to the church, he is clearly seeking the transformation of his bride into something morally and spiritually beautiful (Eph. 5:26–27). This implies that the husband, who is to love like Christ, bears a unique responsibility for the moral and spiritual growth of his wife—which will sometimes require confrontation. If a husband is loving and wise, however, this will feel to a humble wife like she is being served, not humiliated. Christ *died* to purify his bride. Moreover, he goes on speaking to her in his word with a view to applying his sacrifice to her for her transformation. Thus, the wise and loving husband seeks to speak in a way that brings his wife more and more into conformity to Christ.

Similarly, wives are not only submissive wives but also loving sisters. There is a unique way for a submissive wife to be a caring sister—and at times a confronting sister—toward her imperfect brother-husband as she seeks his transformation. She will, from time to time, follow Galatians 6:1 in his case: "If anyone is caught in any transgression, you who are spiritual should restore him in a spirit of gentleness."

Both husband and wife will also obey Matthew 18:15 as necessary, and will do so in the unique demeanor and context called for by headship and submission: "If your brother sins against you, go and tell him his fault, between you and him alone."

Forgiveness and forbearance are the solid foundation on which the call for change can be heard with hope and security rather than fear and a sense of being threatened. Only when a wife or husband feels that the other is totally committed to them—even if he or she doesn't change—can the call for change feel like grace rather than an ultimatum.

So from these and other observations that could be made from the New Testament, I hope it is clear that marriage is not merely forgiving and forbearing. It is also *confronting*—in loving and wise ways formed by the calling of headship and submission.

Talk about It

When was the last time one of you confronted the other in love? Settle it now: you each want to be graciously but clearly confronted when you are on a destructive path—don't you? And who better to do that than your spouse? Each of you give your spouse an open invitation to speak words of truth into your life. Then, in the future, remind each other of that invitation when you get defensive.

25
Loving Difficult People

STACY REAOCH

Bear with one another and, if one has a complaint against another, forgiving each other; as the Lord has forgiven you, so you also must forgive.
—Colossians 3:13

By God's grace, we can keep loving the difficult people God has placed in our lives. The easy thing is to cut the troublesome person out of your life when possible, or just avoid them at best. But I suggest we are more like our patient and loving Savior when we bear with each other and seek to show mercy and kindness, no matter how we are treated.

Here are a six practical ways, among many others, to show love to a difficult person God has placed in your path. This may apply to your marriage right now, but if not, it will before too long. And it definitely will throughout your life when it comes to people outside your marriage—and finding greater peace in relationships outside your marriage will have benefits *within* your marriage.

1. Pray for Your Own Heart

Ask God to soften your heart toward this person, to put off anger and irritability, to put on meekness and kindness, to understand this person's struggles and meet them with compassion (Col. 3:12–14).

2. Pray for Them

Ask God to be at work in their hearts, drawing unbelievers to himself and sanctifying believers to become more like Jesus (Phil. 1:9–11).

3. Move toward Them, Not Away from Them

Although our tendency is to want to steer clear of people with whom we have strained relationships, they are exactly the people we need to be intentionally moving toward. Find ways to engage them in conversation, meet them for coffee, send them a text.

4. Find Specific Ways to Bless and Encourage Them

Write them a note of appreciation. Buy them a book that has been an encouragement to you. Tell them you are praying for them.

5. Give Them Grace, Just as God Extends Grace to You

Remember God's lavish grace poured out for your own daily sins. Ask God to help you bear with them, forgiving them, as he has forgiven you (Col. 3:13).

6. Realize That You Too Could Be the Difficult Person in Someone Else's Life

You might not even realize that you are a thorn in the flesh for someone close to you. Don't be oblivious to your own shortcomings and sins.

So when that child has you on the brink of tears, or you've just received a harsh and critical email, or you're confronted with that extended family member who drives you up the wall, ask God for grace not to run away, but to keep engaging that hard-to-love person with the sacrificial love of Christ.

God will be honored and our hearts will find deeper satisfaction as we seek to love people just as Christ loved us when we were his enemies.

Talk about It

Each of you share with your spouse the one or two people in your life right now who are the most difficult to love. (It may be your spouse; that is not abnormal.) Be honest, and give specific reasons that come to mind. Whoever your "difficult person" is, discuss together how to help each other draw on God's strength to overcome your natural weaknesses.

26

You Are Always in a Temple

JOHN PIPER

I appeal to you therefore, brothers, by the mercies of God, to present your bodies as a living sacrifice, holy and acceptable to God, which is your spiritual worship.
—Romans 12:1

Worship is the term we use to cover all the acts of the heart and mind and body that intentionally express the infinite worth of God. This is what we were created for, as God says in Isaiah 43:7, ". . . everyone who is called by my name, and whom I *have created for my glory.*" That means that we were all created for the purpose of expressing the infinite worth of God's glory. We were created to worship.

But don't think worship *services* when you think worship. That is a huge limitation which is not in the Bible. All of life is supposed to be worship, as we see in Romans 12:1. All of life is lived in the body. And the body is to be presented to God as our "spiritual [service of] worship." This is utterly sweeping. Consider a few implications.

Take breakfast, for example, or Pizza Hut, or mid-morning snacks. First Corinthians 10:31 says, "Whether you eat or drink, or whatever you do, do all to the glory of God." Now eating and drinking are about as basic as you can get. What could be more real and human? We eat and drink every day. We do it at home, at work, in the car, anywhere there is a water fountain. Paul says this all has to do with God. We are to eat and drink in a way that expresses the infinite worth of God. That is quite a challenge, since most eating tends to express the worth of food. How shall we eat so as to worship in our eating?

Or take sex, for example. Paul says the alternative to fornication is worship:

> Flee from sexual immorality. Every other sin
> a person commits is outside the body, but the
> sexually immoral person sins against his own
> body. Or do you not know that your body is a
> temple of the Holy Spirit within you, whom
> you have from God? You are not your own, for
> you were bought with a price. So glorify God in
> your body. (1 Cor. 6:18–20)

Don't fornicate with your body; worship with your body.

He even says that the body is a temple, that is, a place of worship. The body is a place for meeting God, not prostitutes. This doesn't mean sex is bad. It means that sex is precious. Too precious to be treated cheaply. God means for us to put it in a very secure and sacred place—marriage. There it becomes the expression of the love between Christ and the church. It shows the glory of the intensity of God's love for his people. It becomes worship. "Glorify God in your body."

And *not* having sex outside of marriage also shows the preciousness of what it stands for. So chastity is worship. Self-control magnifies Christ above sexuality. And loving sexuality in marriage magnifies Christ as the great lover of his bride, the church (Eph. 5:25–30).

Or take death for a final example. This we will do in our body. In fact, it will be the last act of the body on this earth. The body bids farewell. How shall we worship in that last act of the body? We know we can, because Jesus told Peter how he would die and John said, "This he said to show *by what kind of death he was to glorify God*" (John 21:19). The last deed of the body is to bid farewell to the soul. And our great desire should be that the body bid farewell in a way that expresses the infinite worth of God. The last act should be worship.

How? Paul says in Philippians 1:20–21 that his hope is that Christ will be exalted in his body by death. Then he added, "For to me . . . to die is gain." We express the infinite worth of Christ in dying by counting death as gain. Why gain? Because, verse 23 tells us, that death means going to be "with Christ" which is "far better."

You have a body. But it is not yours. "You were bought with a price. So glorify God in your body." You are always in a temple. Always worship.

Talk about It

Discuss the responsibility and opportunity of all of life being a medium for worship. Ask yourselves how you are doing at worship. Pray together that God would make this true of you as you live your lives together in marriage—in eating, in sex, in all of life, and even in death.

27

You Are Not the Perfect Spouse

JASMINE HOLMES

He who began a good work in you will bring it
to completion at the day of Jesus Christ.
–Philippians 1:6

If the burden of being the perfect spouse rested squarely on our shoulders, our greatest fears about marriage would be completely justified. I just can't be the perfect spouse; neither can you. Praise God that the burden never rested on our shoulders!

Before you were ever married, you were part of the church, the bride of Christ. Before the foundation of the world, our eternal Groom chose us in spite of the fact that we didn't deserve him (Eph. 1:3–4). In the midst of our wretchedness, he died for us (Rom. 5:8). He has clothed us in his righteousness. He adopted us as his own. He saved us. He chose our marriage to echo that eternal covenant love of his Son. He chose us, not because of our perfection, but because of his ability to stand perfectly in our stead. Your lives are his. Your marriage is his.

And in light of these glorious truths, even as our selfishness, self-centeredness, and self-righteousness cry out against the death knells of the old man (Gal. 2:20), we know that final victory belongs to our heavenly Groom (Phil. 1:6). Our weakness points us to his strength (2 Cor. 12:9).

Your marriage isn't ultimate, but it paints, simple as it may be, a picture of the one who is (Rev. 19:7–9), and your greatest fears in marriage can be swallowed by the fact that you are loved not only by your spouse, but even more so by the great Groom who never truly disappoints.

Talk about It

Discuss together your desires, however big or small, to be the perfect spouse to each other, and where you have fallen short. Why is it not only discouraging in one sense, but also good news in another, to discover that you in fact cannot be the perfect spouse?

28

Should My Spouse Talk to Others About Our Marriage Struggles?

JOHN PIPER

Whatever you wish that others would
do to you, do also to them.
—Matthew 7:12

Should spouses talk outside the marriage about problems within the marriage? There are, after all, more or less frequent disappointments in every life, and every marriage faces the normal hardships of getting along when expectations are different. I am not talking here about serious circumstances such as illegal behaviors or life-threatening situations, but common disappointments and challenges. Here are some guidelines.

1) Follow Matthew 18:15, which says that if you find your brother or sister sinning against you or taking a fall, you go to them first. In other words, there is a real effort not to gossip—a real effort not to tell anybody else what you have just seen or found in a person. If this is to apply in the church generally, how much more among spouses? Always start there.

2) The words of Jesus that we do unto others what we would have them do unto us are profoundly significant in marriage (Matt. 7:12). Paul amazingly takes that command and applies it to a husband's love for his wife: "In the same way husbands should love their wives as their own bodies" (Eph. 5:28). It is like "love your neighbor as yourself" (Matt. 19:19) applied to husbands as your own bodies. "He who loves his wife loves himself" (Eph. 5:28).

So Paul draws out the implication not only that we should measure our words and our actions by whether we would want our wives or husbands to treat us that way, but also that, when we treat each other that way, we are really blessing ourselves. We are doing something really good for ourselves not to betray each other's trust.

3) Husbands and wives should observe the biblical principles of reverence and honor. Specifically, because of Ephesians 5:33, wives should think carefully about whether what they say to or about their husbands, in public or in private, is honoring or respectful: "Let each one of you love his wife as himself, and let the wife see that she respects [or reveres] her husband." Similarly, because of 1 Peter 3:7, husbands should think carefully about whether what they say to or about their wives, in public or in

private, honors them as a fellow heir of the grace of life: "Likewise, husbands, live with your wives in an understanding way, showing honor to the woman as the weaker vessel, since they are heirs with you of the grace of life, so that your prayers may not be hindered."

4) We should at times seek permission from our spouses to share the problems of our marriage with one or two very trusted couples or friends that both of us agree on. This point has been so important for my wife and me. We have walked and talked through this numerous times. Often I have asked, "May I share what we talk about with a close friend? May I share what is so frustrating? May I share anything in our relationship that I think would enable him to help me love you better?" That is so different than gossip and venting.

5) Even if you have permission to share specific family issues, you should do it with the greatest of care. Such conversations easily degenerate into simply pouring out our frustrations. A wise friend will call us out on that. We also should ask ourselves whether we are sharing the right amount of detail. Is it too much? It could get very unseemly. Are we sharing in the right tone? Are we using a communication medium that is sufficiently private?

And of course, I am assuming that all of this dialogue will be in a context of praying for and with our spouses and reading Scripture with our spouses so that we seek help from God who alone can keep us married and bring this relationship to a God-honoring, satisfying situation.

Some of these lessons I have had to learn in a very hard way. So I want to encourage you that, if some breach of trust has happened, there is a way forward. There can be repentance and forgiveness. I know that from personal experience.

Talk about It

Discuss your desires and perhaps formulate some simple ground rules for how to draw in a close friend or couple to help with marriage struggles. What are your fears? What benefits might make it worth the risk to draw others into your tensions and conflicts?

29

Pray the Bible Together

DON WHITNEY

Pray without ceasing.
—1 Thessalonians 5:17

What is the method of prayer for most Christians? It's
this: When we pray, we tend to say the same old things
about the same old things. Sooner or later, that kind of
prayer is boring. When prayer is boring, you don't feel like
praying. And when you don't feel like praying, you don't
pray—at least with any fervency or consistency. Prayer
feels much more like duty than delight.

The problem is *not* that we pray *about* the same old
things. To pray about the same things most of the time
is normal. That's because our lives tend to consist of the
same things from one day to the next. Thankfully, dramat-
ic changes in our lives usually don't occur very often.

No, the problem isn't that we pray about the same old things; the problem is that we tend to *say* the same old things about the same old things. The result is that we can be talking to the most fascinating Person in the universe about the most important things in our lives—and be bored to death.

What is the solution? *Pray the Bible.* In other words, slowly read a passage of Scripture and pray about all that comes to mind as you read. Do this, and you'll never again be left to say the same old things in prayer.

Praying the Bible isn't complicated. Read through a few verses of Scripture, pause at the end of each phrase or verse, and pray about what the words suggest to you.

Suppose you are praying your way through Psalm 23. After reading verse one ("The Lord is my shepherd"), you might begin by thanking Jesus for being your Shepherd. Next you might ask him to shepherd your family, making your children or grandchildren his sheep, causing them to love him as their great Shepherd too. After that you might pray for your undershepherds at the church, that Jesus would shepherd them as they shepherd you.

Then, when nothing else comes to mind, you go to the next line, "I shall not want." You might thank him that you've never been in *real* want, or pray for someone—perhaps someone you know, or for a Christian in a place of persecution—who is in want.

You would continue through the psalm until you run out of time. You wouldn't run out of anything to say (if you did, you could just go to another psalm), and best of all, that prayer would probably be unlike any you've ever prayed in your life.

That means if you'll pray the Bible, you'll likely never again say the same old things about the same old things. You don't need any notes or books or any plan to remember. Simply talk to God about what comes to mind as you go line-by-line through his word.

If nothing comes to mind, go to the next verse. If you don't understand that verse, go to the next one. If the following verse is crystal clear, but doesn't prompt anything to pray about, read on. If you want to linger long over a single verse, pray from and about that verse as long as you want.

By this method, your prayers will be guided and shaped by Scripture, and be far more in conformity to the word and will of God than they will if you always make up your own prayers.

Talk about It

Open to Psalm 23, or some other passage of Scripture that comes to mind, and pray together, taking turns reading a verse or two and praying what comes to mind for your marriage and lives together. Consider whether you might make praying the Bible together a daily part of your marriage.

30

Committed to Someone Larger Than Marriage

MARSHALL SEGAL

*Husbands, love your wives, as Christ loved
the church and gave himself up for her.
–Ephesians 5:25*

Marriage is under attack, and I'm not even thinking mainly of so-called "same-sex marriage." Individualism, consumerism, and career-ism have cheapened the perceived value and centrality of marriage. Marriage is now often viewed as simply a convenient social complement to a person's other dreams and ambitions. If it gets difficult or slow or boring or requires more of us than we want, we just withdraw, punish our spouse and kids directly or indirectly, and eventually get out and cut our losses.

Unless, of course, Jesus is the point and power of your marriage. Anyone who has experienced marriage for more than a week will testify that it's hard. That has been true across generations, cultures, and worldviews. Marriages don't survive for decades on comfort and self-fulfillment, at least not happily. Marriages endure and thrive on unchanging, selfless mutual commitment to one another, and to something bigger, stronger, and longer-lasting than the marriage. Christian marriage, therefore, is an opportunity to show the world something—better, Someone—strong enough to keep a marriage together and make it unbelievably meaningful and happy.

Christian marriage declares the gospel more humbly, consistently, and clearly than almost any other kind of relationship we have in this life. That is why God's counsel for marriage is cross-shaped. The path to the most beautiful, most powerful, most satisfying marriages is the road to Calvary. The Bible is clear that the behaviors and rhythms of the marriage covenant are a billboard of Christ's forgiving, sacrificial, redeeming love for sinners. Paul repeats this in several ways, speaking to husbands and wives.

> The husband is the head of the wife even as Christ is the head of the church, his body, and is himself *its Savior*. (Eph. 5:23)

> Husbands, love your wives, as Christ loved the church and *gave himself up for her*. (Eph. 5:25)

"Therefore a man shall leave his father and
mother and hold fast to his wife, and the two
shall become one flesh." This mystery is profound, and I am saying that it refers to *Christ
and the church*. (Eph. 5:31–32)

You rarely see this kind of Christ-like love in other
relationships because the stakes are never as high. A
husband and wife have covenanted before God to love
each other until death. There are no exit ramps or escape
hatches. That might sound scary to some, but we were
made for this kind of love—covenantal, enduring, lavish,
promise-keeping love. It's how God loves us, and it's the
kind of love that confirms—tangibly and regularly—the
gospel we share with our needy world.

Talk about It

Finish this study by discussing what one or two truths
stick out most in your mind and heart from these readings. Pray together that you both would flourish, and your
marriage would thrive, as you rest together in something—Someone—even deeper and bigger than your
marriage.

❈ desiringGod

Everyone wants to be happy. Our website was born and built for happiness. We want people everywhere to understand and embrace the truth that God is most glorified in us when we are most satisfied in him. We've collected more than thirty years of John Piper's speaking and writing, including translations into more than forty languages. We also provide a daily stream of new written, audio, and video resources to help you find truth, purpose, and satisfaction that never end. And it's all available free of charge, thanks to the generosity of people who've been blessed by the ministry.

If you want more resources for true happiness, or if you want to learn more about our work at Desiring God, we invite you to visit us at www.desiringGod.org.

www.desiringGod.org

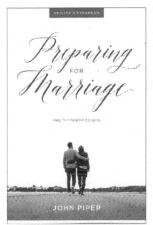

Preparing for Marriage
Help for Christian Couples

by John Piper

As you prepare for marriage, dare to dream with God.

86 pages

Published for Desiring God
by Cruciform Press

bit.ly/prep-for-marriage

When preparing for marriage, or even in just beginning to consider it, it can be immensely helpful to have the perspective of someone like John Piper, not only a seasoned husband of nearly 50 years, but also a seasoned pastor, careful thinker, and faithful theologian.

Chapter 1 includes John's counsel about engagement, **chapter 2** about wedding planning (and finances).

Chapter 3 provides invaluable instruction about the beautiful, complementary dynamic the Bible teaches between husband and wife.

Sexual relations in marriage is the topic of **chapter 4.**

In **chapter 5,** John helps us ponder how we can guard our marriages in a day in which they are under assault from every side.

Chapter 6 is based on perhaps John Piper's single most important message on marriage. There he goes more macro than many of us have ever dared to go in thinking about what marriage is, and what God designed it for. This is a glorious, true, life-changing vision.

Appendix 1 contains almost 50 questions to ask each other, in 11 categories, and **Appendix 2** addresses hospitality.

The Scars That Have Shaped Me
How God Meets Us in Suffering

by Vaneethat Rendall Risner
Foreword by Joni Eareckson Tada

"Raw, transparent, terrifiying, and yet amazingly hopeful!"
Brian Fikkert, co-author of *When Helping Hurts*

200 pages / Published for Desiring God by Cruciform Press

bit.ly/THESCARS

"Vaneetha writes with creativity, biblical faithfulness, compelling style, and an experiential authenticity that draws other sufferers in. Here you will find both a tested life and a love for the sovereignty of a good and gracious God."

John Piper, author of Desiring God *and many other books*

"*The Scars That Have Shaped Me* will make you weep and rejoice not just because it brims with authenticity and integrity, but because every page points you to the rest that is found in entrusting your life to one who is in complete control and is righteous, powerful, wise, and good in every way."

Paul Tripp, pastor, author, international conference speaker

""I could not put this book down, except to wipe my tears. Vaneetha's testimony of God's kindness to her in pain was exactly what I needed; no doubt, many others will feel the same. It has helped me process my own grief and loss, and given me renewed hope to care for those in my life who suffer in various ways."

Gloria Furman, author, **Missional Motherhood; Alive in Him**

"Vaneetha Risner's credibility makes us willing to lean in and listen. Her writing is built on her experience of deep pain, and in the midst of that her rugged determination to hold on to Christ."

Nancy Guthrie, author, **Hearing Jesus Speak into Your Sorrow**

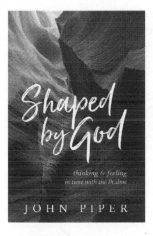

Shaped by God
Thinking and Feeling in Tune with the Psalms

by John Piper

The Psalms are not just commanding...they are contagious.

86 pages

Published for Desiring God
by Cruciform Press

blt.ly/ShapedbyGod

God wants your heart.

The whole Bible teaches truth and awakens emotions, but the Psalms are in a category of their own.

They do not just awaken heart; they put it in the foreground. They do not just invite our emotions to respond to God's truth; they put our emotions on display.

The Psalms are not just commanding; they are contagious. We are not just listening to profound ideas and feelings. We are living among them in their overflow.

We touch pillows wet with tears. We hear and feel the unabashed cries of affliction, shame, regret, grief, anger, discouragement, and turmoil. But what makes all this stunningly different from the sorrows of the world is that all of it—absolutely all of it—is experienced in relation to the totally sovereign God.

This book is an invitation. God wants our hearts. He will take them as he finds them.

And then, with the healing contagion of the Psalms, he will shape them. Accept his invitation to come.

Astonished by God
Ten Truths to Turn the World Upside Down

by John Piper

Turn your world on its head.

192 pages

Published for Desiring God
by Cruciform Press

bit.ly/AstonishedbyGod

For more than thirty years, John Piper pastored in the rough and tumble realities of downtown Minneapolis, preaching his people through the ups and down of life one Sunday at a time. When it came to capturing a generation of joy in one final sermon series, he turned to ten trademark truths to leave ringing in his peoples' ears.

These ten are world-shaking truths—each astonishing in its own way. First they turned Piper's own world upside down. Then his church's. And they will continue to turn the whole world upside down as the gospel of Christ advances in distance and depth. These surprising doctrines, as Piper writes, are "wildly untamable, explosively uncontainable, and electrically future-creating."

Join a veteran author, pastor, and Christian statesman as he captures the ten astonishing, compassionate, life-giving, joy-awakening, hope-sustaining truths that have held everything together for him.